AMERICAN TRAVELER

YOSEMITE
and
The National Parks of California

GALLERY BOOKS
An Imprint of W. H. Smith Publishers Inc.
112 Madison Avenue
New York City 10016

This edition first published in U.S.
in 1991 by Gallery Books,
an imprint of W.H. Smith Publishers, Inc.
112 Madison Avenue, New York, New York 10016

ISBN 0-8317-0258-3

Printed and bound in Spain

For rights information about the photographs in
this book please contact:

The Image Bank
111 Fifth Avenue, New York, NY 10003

Producer: Solomon M. Skolnick
Writer: Elizabeth Tewes
Design Concept: Lesley Ehlers
Designer: Ann-Louise Lipman
Editor: Joan E. Ratajack
Production: Valerie Zars
Photo Researcher: Edward Douglas
Assistant Photo Researcher: Robert V. Hale
Editorial Assistant: Carol Raguso

Title page: *Peaceful moonlight lends a glow to the harsh mountains in Yosemite National Park.* Opposite: *The lacy branches of pine trees provide a dramatic contrast to Yosemite's Half Dome.*

California's five national parks combine to preserve over 1,500,000 acres of land for the enjoyment of people and for the protection of the environment and its animal inhabitants. The creation of these parks spans almost a century, from the setting aside of Sequoia National Park in central California in 1890, to the creation of Channel Islands National Park in southern California in 1980.

These lands not only span an amazing amount of space, they also encompass a dazzling variety of geographic features, rare wildlife, and spectacular and unique flora. They offer visitors the opportunity to enjoy outdoor activities from hiking, swimming, and camping, to skiing, snowshoeing, and mountain climbing. Most of all, they allow everyone to experience the beauty and majesty of the natural world that might have been lost were it not for the unsung conservationists who struggled endlessly and still strive today to protect America's most valuable attribute.

Sparkling blue skies cover the more than 1,000 square miles of Yosemite National Park.

The sheer face of Half Dome towers more than 3,000 feet above the Yosemite Valley. Below: Half Dome's round summit is the result of a process called exfoliation, by which granite sheds its top layers. Opposite: The sheer face of the granite monolith was caused by an ancient glacier cutting away at the mountain's base, causing a section to fall.

Above, left to right: *Yosemite National Park has the world's largest collection of granite domes. The Sierra Nevada, of which the mountains in Yosemite are part, are one long, giant piece of granite.* Below: *A blanket of fog fills the Yosemite Valley, much like a long-ago glacier.* Opposite: *Even when snow covers everything in the valley, Half Dome's south face is still exposed.*

Yosemite

One of the best known and most heavily visited of the parks, Yosemite became a national park in 1890, largely through the efforts of naturalist John Muir, who convinced President Theodore Roosevelt to accompany him on a journey through this wonderful region that crowns the Sierra Nevada.

Most of the three million tourists who pour into the park each year begin their visits in the Yosemite Valley, a seven-mile-long, one-mile-wide swath. Millions of years ago, the entire Yosemite region was covered by a vast, shallow sea which spread as far as the Great Valley of California. The sediments from that sea and from subsequent glaciers and glacial lakes form the flat floor of the valley. Over time, marshland plants colonized the area and were later replaced by grasses, and finally, by trees. Today, some low-lying pockets in the valley still flood each spring and these remain meadows.

The same glaciers which formed the Yosemite Valley also formed small hanging valleys on each side which act as viaducts for several rivers. These rivers shoot down into spectacular waterfalls such as

The beautiful Yosemite Valley was once a great lake, created by melting glaciers which retreated high into the mountains.

Above, left to right: *El Capitan, at the western end of the valley, is the world's largest solid granite rock. Towering 3,604 feet above the valley floor, El Capitan has hardly a crack or a crevice in its sheer face.* Below: *El Capitan's nearly vertical face provides an imposing challenge to rock climbers from all over the world.* Opposite: *The Merced River, which flows through the heart of the Yosemite Valley, reflects the face of El Capitan.*

Yosemite Falls, the highest cataract in North America (2,425 feet), which falls in three great plunges.

Bridalveil Fall drops 620 feet. In a stiff breeze, the water may be diverted as much as 20 feet off the perpendicular. Ribbon Fall (1,612 feet) is also a very light fall and usually dries up near the end of each summer. It is an impressive sight in the spring, however, when its waters make a single plunge of 1,612 feet, the longest single drop in the valley. Other falls include Vernal Fall and Nevada Falls on the Merced River at the east end of the valley, as well as Silver Strand, Staircase, Sentinel, Lehamite, and Illilouette.

Perhaps the most famous, and certainly the most obvious of Yosemite's natural wonders, are the famous peaks of El Capitan and Half Dome. El Capitan, the world's largest exposed granite rock, is, at 3,604 feet, twice the size of the Rock of Gibraltar. Polished by the ancient glaciers, it seems to guard the western end of the valley. The valley floor near El Capitan is nearly free of rocks and boulders since very little debris has ever crumbled from its strong sides.

Preceding pages: *At just a mile wide, the Yosemite Valley is bordered by high granite walls and dotted with boulders and evergreens.* These pages: *Winter snows blanket Yosemite beginning in November, sometimes lasting in the upper region until July.*

Half Dome, at the opposite end of the valley, was formed by a process known as exfoliation. As temperatures change over time, granite sheds its outer layers and reveals a newer layer of rock in the shape of a dome. Solid granite is the only type of rock to form domes in this manner. Half Dome's sheer face, however, was formed in a different way. When glaciers filled the Yosemite Valley, the top of Half Dome remained uncovered. As the glaciers moved down the valley, they undercut the mountain's base and caused part of the mountain to break away.

Preceding page: *Yosemite's famous waterfalls gush forth each spring, but by midsummer, many have dried completely or have slowed to a trickle.* This page, above: *The Lower Yosemite Falls drops 320 feet in a dazzling gush of white water.* Below: *Yosemite Falls, which descends in two levels, is the highest falls in North America at 2,425 feet.*

Bridalveil Fall plunges 620 feet and never runs dry, even at the height of summer. Below: *The diaphanous mist of Bridalveil Fall is often accentuated by a rainbow at the bottom of the cataract.* Opposite: *Sunset turns Horsetail Falls into a dazzling stream of gold.*

Other granite domes such as Sentinel, Liberty Cap, Basket, Turtleback, Mt. Watkins, and Mt. Star King were also formed by exfoliation. Yosemite sports the world's largest collection of these formations because the Sierra Nevada, unlike other mountain ranges, is not a line of individual mountains. Instead, the entire range is one immense chunk of granite that was thrust up from below the earth's crust and tilted west millions of years ago.

Yosemite's meadows offer a pleasing foil to the towering granite mountains. Tuolumne Meadow, located in the northeastern corner of the park, is framed by both jagged and rounded peaks. In spring, which in this high country begins in mid-June, the meadow is covered with wildflowers such as Lemmon's paintbrush, pink shooting star, buttercup, lupine, aster, wallflower, and forget-me-not. The largest alpine meadow in the park, it is the starting point for many backcountry trails as well as some day hikes. In fact, the only way to see most of the remote areas surrounding the Tuolumne Meadow is to hike, because the area is largely roadless.

Above, left to right: *The Merced River drops 317 feet at Vernal Fall. Mist Trail takes hikers close enough to Vernal Fall to feel the spray from the plunging waters.* Below: *Glacier Point, which overlooks the Yosemite Valley 3,000 feet below, also provides a bird's-eye view of Royal Arches.*

After rushing down Nevada and Vernal Falls, the Merced becomes a quiet, glassy river. Below: *Spanish explorers named the river* El Río de Nuestra Señora de la Merced, *meaning "The River of Our Lady of Mercy."*

The Tuolumne Meadow is bisected by the lovely Tuolumne River. To the west of the meadow, the river runs through a mile-deep gorge called the Grand Canyon of the Tuolumne River. Near the head of the canyon rushes Waterwheel Falls, which, like most of the park's falls, are most impressive in the late spring when runoff from the melting snow on the mountain peaks floods the waterways.

The Hetch Hetchy Reservoir is just west of the Grand Canyon of the Tuolumne River. Once a pristine valley, it was flooded in 1913 when the O'Shaugnessy Dam was completed. Today, the valley stands under water 300 feet deep.

Yosemite also contains three separate groves of giant sequoias, the most popular of which is the Mariposa Grove of Big Trees. This 205-acre grove contains approximately 500 gigantic redwood trees. The largest of these is the Grizzly Giant, which is more than 200 feet tall and has a circumference of about 96 feet. It is estimated to be at least 3,800 years old. The grove also contains two tunnel trees, through which visitors may drive their cars.

Although the redwoods are the oldest trees now living, they are closely followed by the western, or Sierra, juniper. Growing on the harsh sides of the granite mountains, the western juniper is a heavy-limbed evergreen. Its branches are twisted and gnarled and look much like driftwood that has been weathered by the sea and salt air. Despite the brutal environment in which these trees grow, they can live as long as 2,000 years.

Preceding page: *Ice chokes the Merced River as it flows toward Cathedral Rocks in the distance.* This page, above: *Visitors to Yosemite can make trips to Tenaya Lake on foot or on horseback.* Below: *Tenaya Lake is named for the chief of a tribe of Native Americans which inhabited the region until the mid-1800's.*

Preceding page: *Trees appear to grow straight out of solid rock on Olmsted Point, but their roots cling to small fissures in the surface.* This page, above: *A juniper and a dwarf Jeffrey pine have taken root in the harsh environment of Olmsted Point. Below, left to right: Huge boulders perch where passing glaciers deposited them. Tioga Pass winds its way through the High Sierras.*

The trees in Yosemite vary according to their various environments. What makes the forests of Yosemite particularly special is the fact that most of them have never been logged and few areas have been the victims of recent fires. Approximately one-fifth of the park is a mixed conifer forest including incense cedar, ponderosa and sugar pine, Douglas and white fir. One-quarter of the park is a red fir forest, which may also include lodgepole and Jeffrey pine. Pure stands of lodgepole do occur, but they are often found in stands mixed with western white pine, mountain hemlock, and whitebark pine, as well as with the red firs.

While the virgin forests and the unique geography are reasons enough to sing the praises of Yosemite, many visitors are drawn to the park for the opportunity to view wildlife in its natural habitat. Bird-watchers are particularly fascinated with this region in which more than 220 different species have been identified. The rufous hummingbird, acorn woodpecker, mountain chickadee, western tanager, gray-crowned rosy finch, and many others inhabit the park.

The western, or Sierra, juniper reaches out its gnarled branches while its roots hold it firmly to the rocky outcropping. Although seemingly precariously perched, this tree may have been here for as long as 2,000 years.

Although Yosemite has three stands of giant sequoias, the Mariposa Grove near the
south entrance has the largest concentration of trees—500 mature specimens.
Opposite: *The Grizzly Giant in the Mariposa Grove is approximately 209 feet tall and
is estimated to be almost 4,000 years old.*

Present, too, are more than 25 species of reptiles and amphibians, the most common of which may be the mountain yellow-legged frog. But many visitors do not feel their trip is complete without seeing at least one of the large mammals that make the park their home.

Raccoons, yellow-bellied marmots, California gray squirrels, and chubby Belding's ground squirrels are all common in the park. Less common are the California mule deer, black bear, coyote, mountain lion, and wolverine. Recently reintroduced to the park are Sierra bighorn sheep.

This page, top to bottom: *Although most visitors won't see them, coyotes are residents of the park. The mule deer, named for its large, mule-like ears, is the park's most abundant large mammal, commonly seen in the early morning or late afternoon foraging for food in meadows. Bighorn sheep, once decimated by diseases carried by domestic sheep grazing in and near the park, have recently been reintroduced to the area. Opposite: While bobcats generally hunt at night, they may occasionally be seen sunning themselves in out-of-the-way areas.*

Sequoia and Kings Canyon

Sequoia National Park, the second oldest in the U.S., was established in October 1890. Kings Canyon, by contrast, was established in 1940. However, since they are adjacent to each other, they are administered as one unit and most visitors, while concentrating on either, generally see at least some sites in both.

The attraction of both parks is that they contain the largest specimens of *Sequoiadendron gigantea*, giant sequoia. The biggest of these is the General Sherman tree. Although at 275 feet it is not the tallest, it is the most massive in terms of bulk. It is estimated to weigh 4.5 million pounds and may be as much as 2,600 years old. The General Grant tree, from which Grant Grove takes its name, is almost as large as the General Sherman tree at 267 feet and is very nearly as old. Congress declared it the nation's Christmas tree and each year services are held beneath its boughs to celebrate both Christmas and another year in the life of these amazing plants.

Although the General Sherman and the General Grant trees may be the most famous individual trees, the

Rushing streams and granite mountains characterize Sequoia and Kings Canyon in the Sierra Nevada south of Yosemite.

Lone Pine Creek, pictured here, just barely grazes the edge of Sequoia National Park; it is actually a part of the adjacent Inyo National Forest. Below: Big Bird Lake, at the south end of Deadman Canyon, reflects the surrounding granite walls.

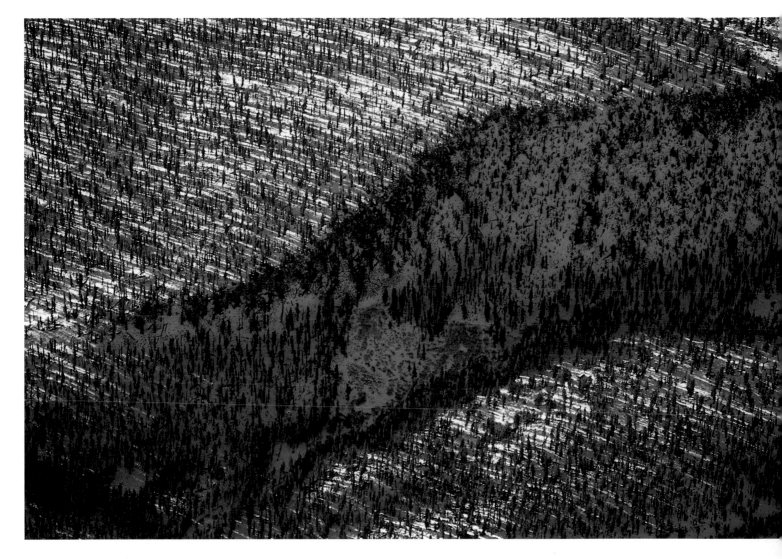

Triple Divide Peak and the surrounding mountains in the center of Sequoia National Park are covered with idyllic forests and, in winter, a deep layer of snow.

400 steps lead to the top of Moro Rock, a 6,725-foot monolith that rears up from the edge of Giant Forest. Opposite: Although they are not the tallest trees, giant sequoias are the largest living things in the world, with an almost unimaginable bulk.

Preceding page: *The General Sherman tree is the largest of all, with a trunk diameter of over 30 feet and a weight of approximately 4.5 million pounds.* This page, above: *One reason giant sequoias live so long and grow so big is that they are almost impervious to disease, fire, and lightning because their thick, spongy bark acts as a protective cloak.* Below: *Giant sequoias are susceptible to erosion and sometimes simply topple over because their roots do not provide sufficient anchorage.*

parks contain the most exten-
sive groves of giant sequoias
in the world. The growth is
the most dense in the Giant
Forest, where visitors may see
all the phases of life from tiny
seedlings to huge trees that
have fallen in storms.

Although they are gener-
ally impervious to lightning
and insects because of their
thick, spongy bark, they are
particularly susceptible to
erosion. Lacking the deep tap
roots of other large trees, the
sequoias have a very shallow
system of feeder roots, which
can spread for more than 100
feet. However, these roots do
little to anchor the tree, which
can easily fall in a storm.

Impressive as the trees
may be, their size pales in
comparison to Mt. Whitney on
the eastern edge of Sequoia
National Park. The highest
peak in the contiguous U.S., it
towers to 14,495 feet.

There are wonderful
sights to behold below ground
as well. Crystal Cave, a small

Preceding pages, left: *On some giant
sequoias, their towering majesty is
enhanced by the fact that their lowest
branch is 100 feet off the ground.*
Right: *The John Muir Trail starts at
Sequoia's Mt. Whitney and winds
218 miles through the high country
all the way to the Yosemite Valley.*
These pages: *Although now puffy
white and violet, the clouds over the
Sierra Nevada range can quickly
change to ominous storm clouds.*

These bare pine trees in Kings Canyon National Park provide an interesting foil to the dark blue sky in the background. Below: *Like Yosemite to the north, Kings Canyon has its share of impressive domes which rise up like sentinels from valley floors.*

marble cavern, delights visitors with an underground stream and smooth stalactites and stalagmites.

In a region well known for its breathtaking landscapes, Kings Canyon is truly wonderful. The deepest canyon in North America, it plunges as deep as 8,000 feet from the top of the ridge to the rushing waters. The narrow, V-shaped canyon is bordered by granite walls and steep cliffs.

Lassen Volcanic

Although Lassen Volcanic became a national park in 1916, the region gained national attention in 1915 when Lassen Peak erupted. Today Lassen is dormant, but that eruption is still evident in the part of the park known as the Devastated Area. Completely denuded of every tree, shrub, and blade of grass by the volcanic blast, the area now sports a young pine forest.

Lassen Volcanic's Bumpass Hell is an another area that owes its fame to volcanic activity. Hot springs, mud pots, and fumaroles gurgle as a result of underground turbulence. The odor of sulphur fills the air, while bright red, yellow, and black algae flourish in the water, which can reach temperatures of 196 degrees.

Lassen Volcanic has many other thermal features. Sulphur Works, Vulcan's Castle, Devil's Kitchen, and Boiling Springs Lake all hiss and

This page, top to bottom: *This trail marker near Bumpass Hell in Lassen Volcanic National Park reminds visitors of the dangers of not respecting nature's more furious displays; while the earth here looks solid enough, it may not support an incautious visitor's weight. Visitors to Lassen can smell Bumpass Hell before they see it; the odor of sulphur from the fumaroles, mud pots, and boiling springs carries a great distance. Although the water in a boiling spring may reach almost 200 degrees, brightly colored algae thrive in the scalding waters.*

bubble with hot water and steam. Even during the coldest of winters, when Lassen Peak is covered with up to 50 feet of snow, the thermal features continue to warm the air around them.

Lassen's position on the Pacific Ring of Fire is responsible for all the volcanic activity. While hot springs, eruptions, and mud pots are the result of such explosive energy, so too is peaceful Manzanita Lake. About 300 years ago, three volcanic mountains exploded, setting off a series of avalanches. As a result, many nearby streams were dammed and Manzanita Lake was created.

Although snow blankets the usually black Cinder Cone in winter, the nearby thermal features keep the ground clear year-round. Below: These signs explain the geologic forces which led to the violent eruption of Lassen Peak in 1915, one year after it began to spew steam and ash.

Lassen Peak, one of the volcanoes on the Pacific Ring of Fire, was named for pioneer Peter Lassen, who guided parties of settlers to California. Below: Lassen Peak Trail starts at an elevation of 8,512 feet and winds its way to the summit at 10,457 feet.

The region of Cinder Cone, a giant pile of black volcanic ash, is the result of yet another eruption. For years, Cinder Cone was able to erupt freely, sending lava and ash into the air. Over time, the ash settled back around the cone and was blown into deposits now called the Painted Dunes.

Several Native American tribes lived in this region well into the mid-1800s. But with the California gold rush came many new settlers and the Yana, Maidu, and Atsugewi were forced out. In time, only seven Yahis, a group related to the Yana, remained. In 1911, Ishi, the last of the Yahis, came out of the mountains and was eventually befriended by anthropologists from the University of California.

Although Ishi had never been to the top of Lassen Peak because his people thought a visit might anger the god who lived there, he led an expedition of scientists to the summit in 1913. The following year, Lassen began to stir, and in 1915, the entire top of the mountain blew apart.

Unlike the hot waters of such thermal features as Boiling Springs Lake, the waters of King's Creek Falls run white and cold. Overleaf: On a clear day from the summit of Lassen Peak, it's possible to see all the way to Mt. Shasta, over 50 miles away.

Redwood

Established in 1968, Redwood National Park preserves more than a 40-mile stretch of redwood forest, bordered on the west by the Pacific Ocean and on the east by mountains. Once stretching for nearly 500 miles, and extending inland as far as 20 miles, the old-growth forest is the sight of the world's tallest living thing, a giant at 370 feet. Also in the same region, called Tall Trees Grove, stand the second- and third-tallest trees.

Although the magnificent redwoods are the most well known attractions in the park, many visitors are pleasantly surprised by Fern Canyon. In this park where big is best, the ferns in Fern Canyon may grow up to fifty feet tall. Too shady for most trees and flowers to grow, the canyon provides a carpet of cool mosses for hikers who wander among the leafy fronds.

Cool Pacific waters lap at the shores of Redwood National Park in northern California. Below: Fern Canyon boasts many different varieties of ferns, which grow to stupendous sizes in an area that is too shady for most other plants. Opposite: The coast redwoods awe visitors not just because of their height and girth, but because of their beauty.

BIG TREE

	FT	MTRS
HEIGHT	304	92.6
DIAMETER	21.6	6.6
CIRCUMFERENCE	68	20.7
ESTIMATED AGE	1500 YRS	

Although Redwood National Park is known mostly for the giant trees, mosses and ferns also love the cool, wet environment. Below, left to right: *The brilliant foliage of the vine maple adds some crimson to the mostly green landscape. Gigantism is not confined to the redwoods: various types of rhododendron also grow in this region, some reaching heights of nearly 40 feet.*

But it is perhaps the coast that is most rewarding. From a vantage point on the rocks, visitors can look inland to see the giant redwoods seemingly marching straight into the wild, foaming sea. In December, they can look westward to see 45-foot-long gray whales migrating south to warm waters, while harbor seals bask on land during low tide.

A fiery sunset makes striking silhouettes of the trees in Redwood National Park. Below: Mist shrouds a grove of trees in the park; almost a rain forest, the park may receive 100 inches or more of rain each year.

Channel Islands

Consisting of five islands off the coast of southern California, Channel Islands National Park boasts mountains, rocky coves, sand dunes, freshwater springs, fog, and rolling hills, as well as an astounding variety of flora and fauna.

San Miguel, the westernmost island, is a refuge for six different types of seals. Harbor seals, Steller sea lions, Guadeloupe fur seals, and northern fur seals all stop in at the island. For the California sea lion and the northern elephant seal, it is an important breeding ground.

West Island (one of the three small islands that make up Anacapa) is the site of the only permanent colony of brown pelicans, an endangered species, on the West Coast of the U.S.

Santa Cruz, the largest island, was once the home of members of the seafaring Chumash tribe, who fished and hunted sea otters and seals. Today their culture is known from the excavated ruins of their villages.

This page, top to bottom: *Frequent visitors to Channel Islands National Park, a mother harbor seal rests on shore while her baby takes a swim. These young California sea lions, also common in the islands, gather together to nap in the sun. Inflatable air channels in the bull elephant seal's snout amplify its bellows; the sound can be heard almost a mile away.* Opposite: *Anacapa Island, really a collection of three small islands, catches the rising sun.*

An even more impressive archaeological site is found on Santa Rosa. Scientists have discovered the remains of a dwarf mammoth in a fire pit which has been estimated to be 35,000 years old, indicating that humans have been in North America for at least that long.

Santa Barbara is known primarily for the profusion of wildflowers which blanket the island. Although it boasts no fresh water except from rain, the island is graced by giant yellow coreopsis, a relative of the sunflower.

The national parks of California offer an unequalled bounty to visitors and inhabitants alike. These parks preserve unique ecosystems, endangered species, geological wonders, and exotic flora. They offer the opportunity for solitude, education, conservation, and entertainment. Spanning the state, these parks are a legacy of the wilderness that once spanned the continent.

Preceding pages, left: *All of the islands, including Santa Rosa (pictured here), are covered with wildflowers each spring.* Right: *Calich fossils such as this one are formed when a plant, covered by wind-driven sand, dies and leaves an empty shell. San Miguel Island boasts dozens of these fossils on its sand dunes.* These pages: *Taken from Inspiration Point on East Anacapa Island, Middle and West Anacapa Islands stand out against the setting sun in this photograph.*

Index of Photography

All photographs courtesy of The Image Bank except where indicated *.